A FEW TIPS FOR ADULTS:

Allow your children to work at their own pace and respect their "refusals"!
If they close the book or skip a page, it doesn't necessarily mean they're giving up.
They may just need a little time to think about how to solve the problems.

Ask questions rather than give answers!
If your child asks you for help, don't give them the answer. Rather, help them focus
on the problem, or their mistake, by asking targeted questions.

Let your children find their own way to solve the problems, even if it's long
and convoluted. You can then help them explore other, perhaps more "clever," ways
to find solutions.

Understanding is the first step to problem-solving.
Help your children work through the problems before trying to solve them.
You can do this by verbalizing, drawing the steps, or using real objects.
This is the easiest, yet least fun part of problem-solving!

Ask "How did you do that?"
Gradually help them get accustomed to verbalizing and explaining
their thinking processes; it's far more important for them to know how
and why they came up with an answer than to know the name of the rule applied.

The situations proposed in this book are of course imaginary.
Help your children discover numbers and math in everyday life.
Get your nose out of the book and go and find math!

BLACK BUBBLES!

In the Ocean of Sums, an octopus and a starfish hover between the rocks on the Math Coral Reef, staring apprehensively at the water in front of them.
"Aster, can you see them?"
"Yes, Olly. They're terrifying!"
For the past few days, there's been a stream of oily bubbles in the ocean. They are blacker than the night and as big as watermelons, and everything they touch disappears. Numerical rocks, math fish, and other reef dwellers...Poof! They're gone. Swallowed up by the sticky black bubbles.
"I bet it was someone who hates math," grumbles Olly, crossing his tentacles in frustration.
"Yeah, they're polluting the ocean and damaging everything with this black stuff." "You're right, Aster. They're up to no good."
Bob the rockfish suddenly peeps out from the rocks. "Hi, Aster, are you alone?"
"No, Olly's here."
"Olly? Where is he?"
You see, if it wasn't for his eyes, no one would even know that the octopus was there.
"I'm here!" says Olly, changing color so they can see him.
"Have you seen how many there are?" In fact, the black bubbles are multiplying as they speak.
"They're going to end up poisoning the ocean and erasing all the numbers and sums!" Bob says to his friends.
"Yeah," replies Olly. "Well, I'm not going to stand around and watch that happen."
"What do you mean?"
"Let's find out where the bubbles are coming from and stop them."
"Good idea! But where do we start?"
"We could follow the bubbles backwards."
"Will it be a long journey?" asks Aster.
"It could be. Why?"
"Well...we'll need to make sure we have enough snacks!"

LET'S GET SUPPLIES!

LIKE ALL STARFISH, **ASTER IS VERY HUNGRY**. HELP HER STOCK UP WITH ENOUGH FOOD FOR THE JOURNEY. SHE CAN EAT EVERYTHING THAT EQUALS 12.

4 X 3 =
6 X 2 =
2 X 3 =
8 ÷ 8 =
8 + 3 =
6 + 7 =
14 - 2 =
3 + 9 =
8 + 4 =
7 - 2 =
9 - 2 =
12 ÷ 1 =
6 + 6 =
10 + 2 =
6 + 5 =
5 X 3 =
10 - 2 =
2 X 7 =
20 - 8 =
2 X 5 =
5 + 7 =
2 + 8 =
1 + 11 =

WHICH WAY SHALL WE GO?

TOWARD THE PLUS CORAL MEADOWS, THE MINUS CLIFFS, OR THE DIVIDING ABYSS? TO FIND THE RIGHT WAY, FOLLOW THE BOXES WITH THE **SUMS THAT EQUAL 6, 12, OR 14**.

	2 + 4 =	4 - 4 =
2 + 8 =	5 + 9 =	5 - 3 =
9 + 4 =	8 + 4 =	8 + 5 =
6 + 1 =	6 + 8 =	7 + 8 =
5 + 2 =	5 + 1 =	9 + 3 =
	6 + 4 =	7 + 4 =

MINUS CLIFFS

10 + 3 =

5 + 4 =

PLUS CORAL MEADOWS

12 + 3 =

6 + 5 =

7 + 6 =

8 + 2 =

5 + 5 =

9 + 8 =

3 + 4 =

10 + 5 =

9 + 1 =

11 + 3 =

4 + 8 =

4 + 3 =

6 + 7 =

9 + 5 =

DIVIDING ABYSS

"THE BUBBLES ARE COMING FROM THE ...."
"WE'LL HAVE TO CROSS THE MATH CORAL REEF TO GET THERE!" EXCLAIMS ASTER.

THE MATH CORAL REEF IS BRIMMING WITH LIFE AND SUMS

LOTS OF DIFFERENT SPECIES COME HERE TO MULTIPLY, GET TOGETHER, OR EAT A SNACK.
BELOW ARE ALL THE FISH OUR FRIENDS ENCOUNTER.

HOW MANY FISH OF EACH SPECIES DO THEY MEET?
COUNT THEM AND ADD THEM UP.

SPECIES	SCENE 1	SCENE 2	SCENE 3	SCENE 4	TOTAL

 CLARA IS A CLOWN FISH, AND SHE LAYS HER EGGS ON THE MATH CORAL REEF. **SOLVE THE ADDITION PROBLEM** ON EACH ROCK, AND THEN ATTACH THE STICKERS (AT THE BACK OF THE BOOK) WITH THE CORRECT NUMBER OF EGGS THAT CLARA LAYS.

WHO BELONGS TO WHO?

HELP THE PARENTS FIND THEIR NESTS BY MATCHING THE EGGS TO THEIR RESPECTIVE FISH-ADDENDS, AS SHOWN IN THE EXAMPLE. COUNT THE SCALES ON THE FISH: THE **SUM OF THE SCALES** ON BOTH PARENTS MUST BE EQUAL TO THE NUMBER OF **EGGS**.

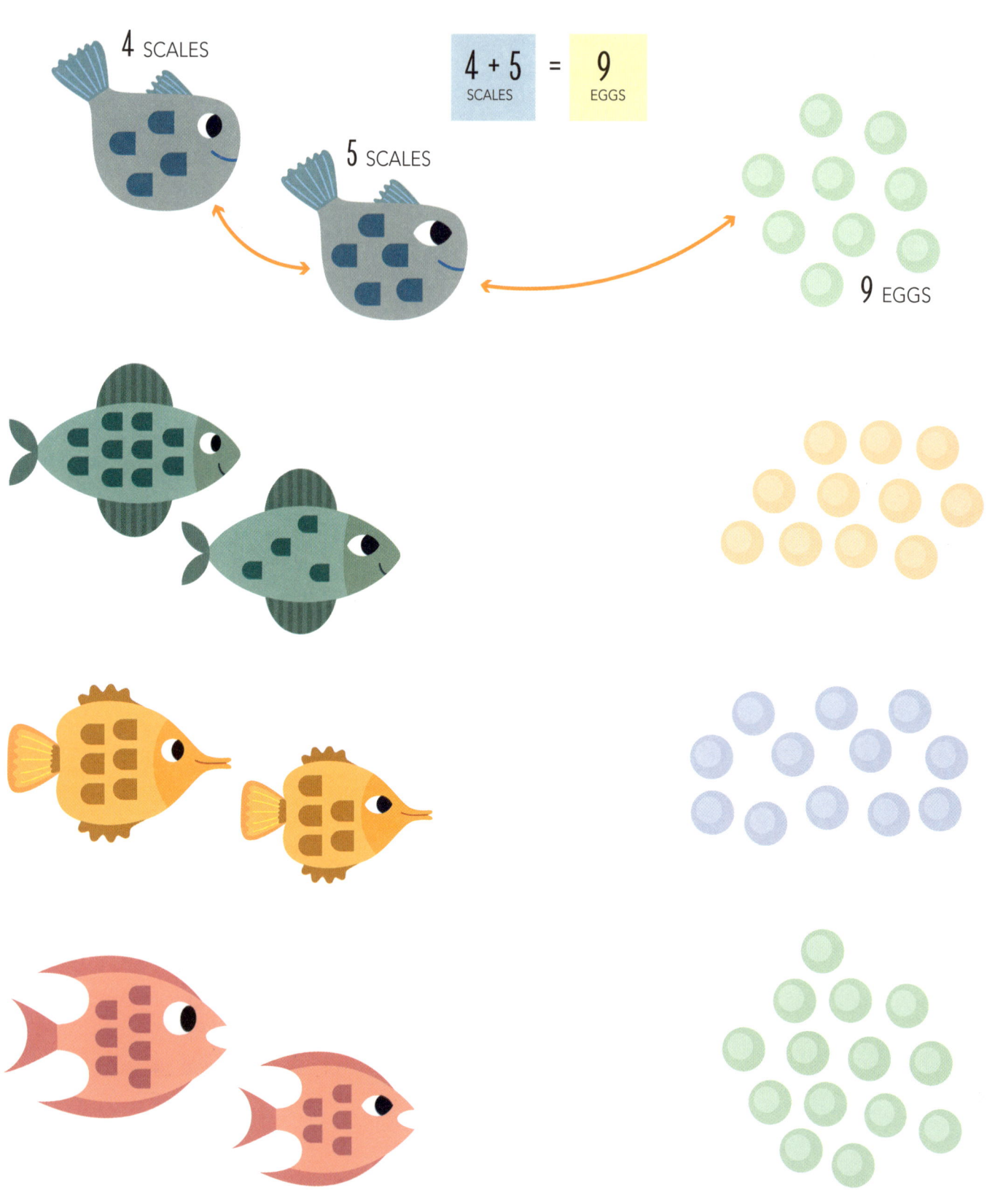

A MULTICOLORED CORAL REEF

"THIS CORAL REEF IS **SO COLORFUL!**" EXCLAIMS ASTER ENTHUSIASTICALLY. "ISN'T IT, OLLY?" THE OCTOPUS SCOWLS AT HER: JUST AS HE MANAGES TO CAMOUFLAGE HIMSELF, HE HAS TO CHANGE COLOR AGAIN. "THIS IS REALLY STRESSING ME OUT," COMPLAINS OLLY. HELP THE OCTOPUS FEEL LESS LIKE A MOLLUSK OUT OF WATER BY SOLVING THE PROBLEMS AND **COLORING THE SPACES WITH THE CORRECT COLOR.**

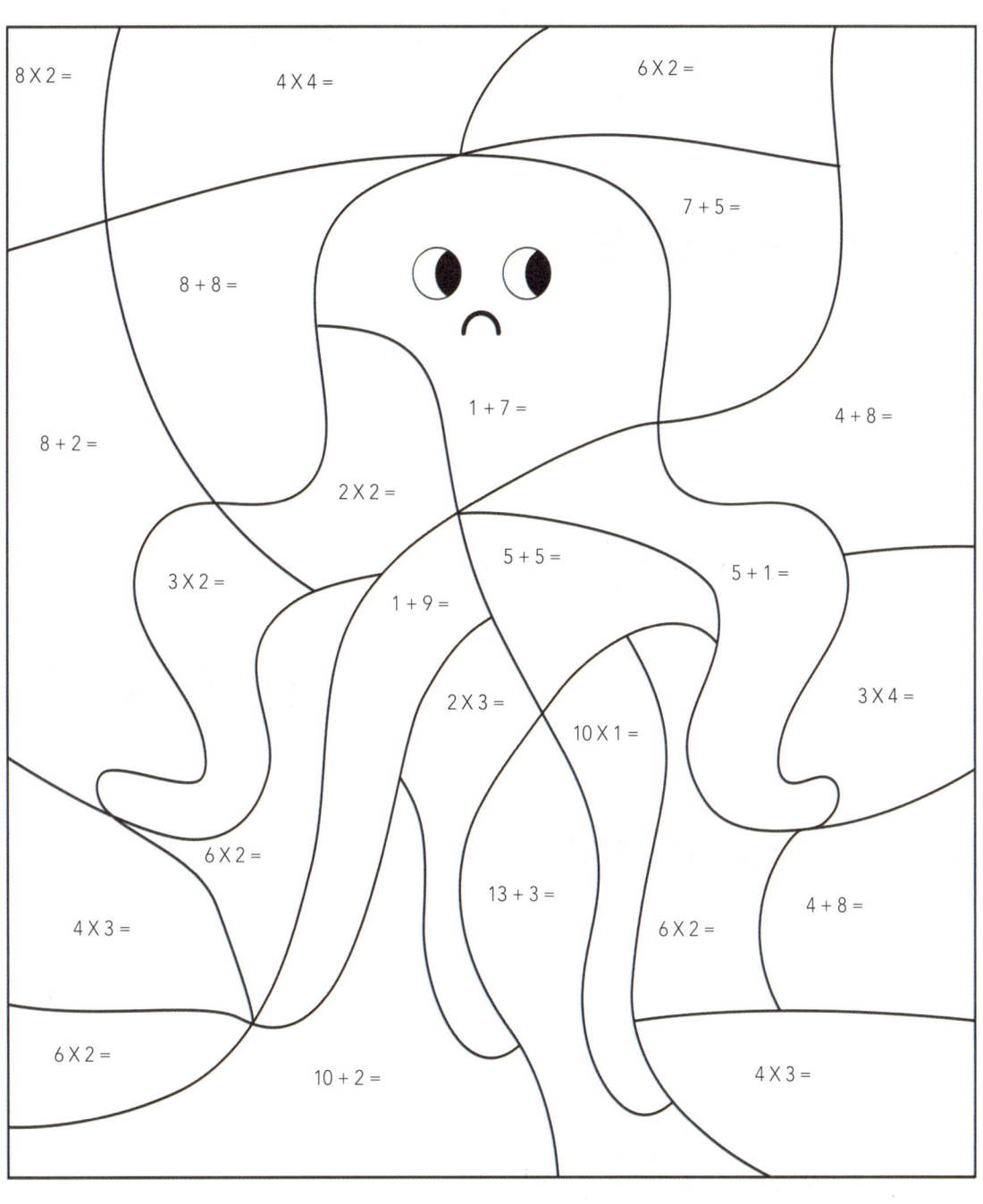

| 4 | 6 | 8 | 10 | 12 | 16 |

PREDATORS AND PREY

"THERE ARE **PREDATORS** TO KEEP THE NUMBER OF FISH ON THE REEF UNDER CONTROL, WHICH IS VERY IMPORTANT FOR THE HEALTH OF AN ECOSYSTEM. ISN'T THAT RIGHT, ASTER?...ASTER? YOU'D EAT SNACKS ALL DAY IF YOU COULD!" SAYS OLLY KNOWINGLY. **CROSS OUT THE MUSSELS THAT ASTER EATS** AND THEN SUBTRACT THEM, AS SHOWN IN THE EXAMPLE.

9 - 3 = 6

6 - 4 =

7 - 5 =

8 - 1 =

9 - 7 =

5 - 4 =

8 - 6 =

7 - 1 =

8 - 2 =

BUT THERE ARE FAR MORE PREDATORS

USE THE STICKERS AT THE BACK OF THE BOOK TO COMPLETE THE EMPTY SPACES ON THE PYRAMIDS OF WHO EATS WHO. **THE TOP TILE IS THE SUM OF THE TWO TILES BELOW,** AS IN THE EXAMPLE BELOW.

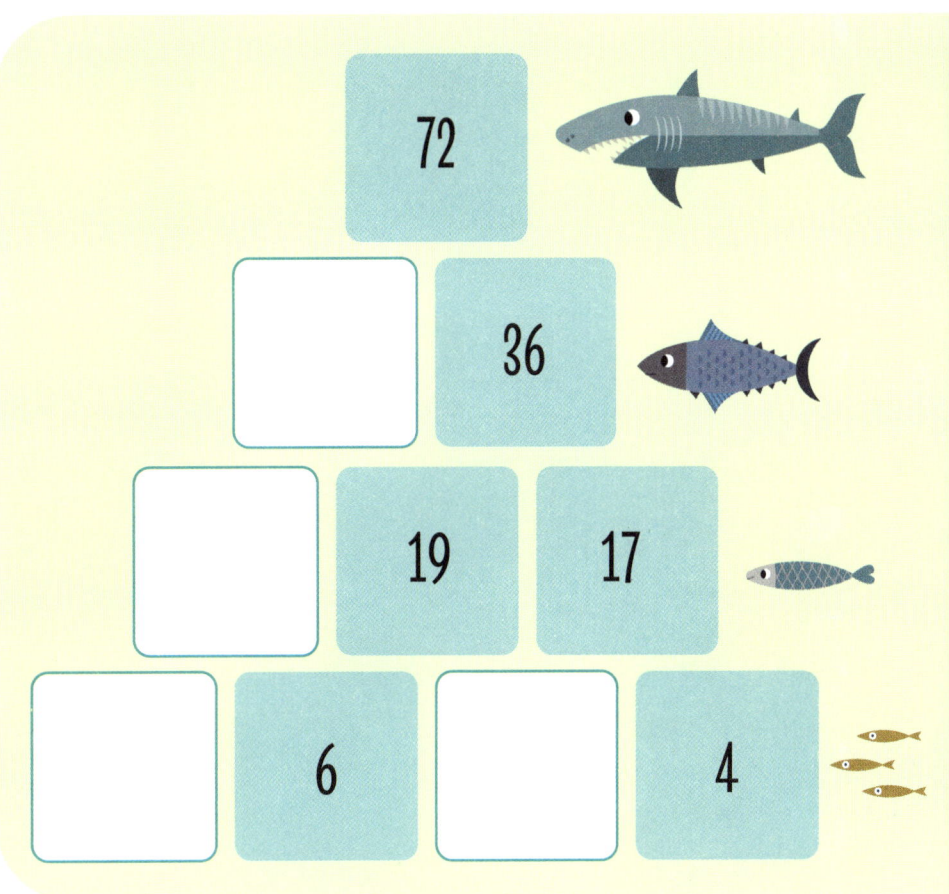

8 + 2 = 10

LET'S REPAIR THE CORAL REEF

"ARE WE GOING THE RIGHT WAY?" ASKS ASTER. "UNFORTUNATELY, I THINK WE ARE," SIGHS OLLY, PUTTING HIS TENTACLES ON HIS HEAD. "LOOK. IT'S FULL OF **BLACK HOLES!** THE BUBBLES HAVE DONE A LOT OF DAMAGE HERE. WE SHOULD DO SOMETHING TO HELP." HELP REPAIR THE MATH CORAL REEF BY SOLVING THE PROBLEMS AND COMPLETING THE CROSSWORD.

THE JOURNEY CONTINUES
OLLY, BOB, AND ASTER CONTINUE ON THEIR JOURNEY: HELP THEM FIND A **SAFE ROUTE** BY ATTACHING THE CORRECT STEP-COUNTING STICKERS.

THE EDGE OF THE CORAL REEF

"THE CORAL REEF ENDS HERE," WHISPERS BOB, INDICATING THE OPEN OCEAN WITH ONE OF HIS FINS.
"WE'RE ALMOST AT THE DIVIDING ABYSS!"
"THAT MAY BE," SIGHS OLLY, "BUT GETTING THERE IS GOING TO BE DANGEROUS. AND NOT JUST BECAUSE OF THE BUBBLES," HE CONTINUES IN A LOW VOICE.
"COME ON, GUYS!" SAYS ASTER. "WE'LL BE STEALTHY. NO ONE WILL EVEN KNOW WE'RE HERE. BUT ALL OF US HAVE TO GO OVER THE WAVES USING OUR OWN **SECRET CODE!**"

THE DIVIDING ABYSS

Aster, Bob, and Olly see a strange creature crawling among the rocks.
"Hey, what's that?"
"It's a tasty crustacean," whispers Aster happily. "I do actually feel quite hungry," says Olly, nodding. "Don't get distracted...," starts Bob, but before he can finish the sentence, Aster and Olly have already swum off. "Oh well. I suppose it is time for a snack." The victim soon finds himself entangled in tentacles and tube feet.
"NO! DON'T EAT ME! DO YOU WANT TO CROSS THE ABYSS? IT'S REALLY DANGEROUS! I CAN HELP YOU!"
"What's dangerous?" ask the two very hungry friends.
"CROSSING IT," replies the unfortunate crustacean.
"Let him go!" snaps Bob. "Sorry, what's your name?"
"Todd the Isopod."
"Let go of Todd! Can you explain yourself better?"
"The Giant Crab and the Herring King are fighting to become the Lords of the Dividing Abyss. It's impossible to cross it without taking sides. But I know how to. So, please don't eat me."
"Okay!" replies Bob, glaring at Aster and Olly. "We are not going to eat Todd for lunch." Reluctantly, Aster and Olly let go of him. "Will you be our guide?" they ask him.
"Yes, of course!"

THE EDGE OF THE CORAL REEF

IT'S PITCH BLACK. SUDDENLY, A LIGHT GOES ON, AND ASTER AND OLLY FIND THEMSELVES SURROUNDED. ON THE LEFT, THERE'S A **GIANT CRAB**. ON THE RIGHT, A VERY LONG FISH WITH TWO COLORFUL CRESTS: THE **HERRING KING**. AND WITH THEM, THERE IS AN ARMY OF DEEP-SEA CREATURES. TODD APPEARS FROM THE SHADOWS. "THESE ARE THE PLAYERS YOU REQUESTED, YOUR MAJESTY."
"YOU'RE A HORRIBLE ISOPOD!" HISSES ASTER. "YOU LIED TO US."

FORM YOUR TEAMS

THE GAME TO SEE WHO WILL BECOME LORD OF THE ABYSS IS ABOUT TO BEGIN. UNFORTUNATELY, ASTER AND OLLY FIND THEMSELVES ON **DIFFERENT TEAMS**. FIND THE RIGHT POSITION FOR EACH PLAYER BY COUNTING THE COLORED SQUARES, AND THEN **ATTACH THE CORRESPONDING STICKERS TO THE BATTLEFIELD**. THE GIANT CRAB TEAM'S ANSWERS ARE **MULTIPLES OF 3**. THE HERRING KING TEAM'S ANSWERS ARE **MULTIPLES OF 5**.

LET THE FIRST CHALLENGE BEGIN!

"IT'S TIME FOR THE GAMES TO START," ANNOUNCES THE GIANT CRAB, SNAPPING HIS HUGE CLAWS. "IS EVERYBODY READY?"
"JUST A MINUTE," INTERRUPTS ASTER. "I DON'T KNOW WHAT I'M SUPPOSED TO DO."
"A MATH COMPETITION, OF COURSE! THE GREAT STARFISH CHALLENGE."

COMPLETE THE PROBLEMS SO THAT EACH ANSWER IS THE SAME AS THE NUMBER IN THE MIDDLE OF THE STARFISH.

Starfish 1 (center 8):
- X 2
- 16 ÷
- − 9
- 6 +
- 5 +

Starfish 2 (center 15):
- X 3
- 30 ÷
- 11 +
- 6 +
- + 7

Starfish 3 (center 12):
- X 2
- ÷ 3
- − 4
- + 6
- 9 +

THIS IS THE RIGHT CHALLENGE FOR ME!

THE SPERM WHALES

NOW SOLVE THE SPERM WHALE PUZZLE!
WHAT DID THE SPERM WHALE EAT?
COMPLETE ALL THE PUZZLES WITH EITHER NUMBERS OR DRAWINGS, USING THE EXAMPLE AS A GUIDE.

TIME FOR THE TONGUE FISH GAME!

THINGS ARE REALLY HEATING UP! TO PLAY YOU'LL NEED: A PENCIL, TWO DICE, THE STICKERS AT THE BACK OF THE BOOK, AND A WORTHY OPPONENT (ASK A FRIEND!).

AFTER THE FIRST MATCH, PLAY AGAIN USING PEBBLES OR SOMETHING ELSE AS TOKENS!

1

CHOOSE YOUR TEAM: THE **GIANT CRAB** OR THE **HERRING KING**.

2

CHOOSE FOUR DIFFERENT NUMBERS BETWEEN 0 AND 12, THEN WRITE THEM IN THE WHITE BOXES ON THE **TONGUE FISH**.

3

TAKE TURNS ROLLING THE DICE. YOU CAN EITHER ADD OR SUBTRACT THE NUMBERS YOU ROLL.
IF THE ANSWER TO THE PROBLEM MATCHES ONE OF THE WRITTEN NUMBERS, ATTACH ONE OF YOUR TEAM'S STICKERS NEXT TO THE BASE.

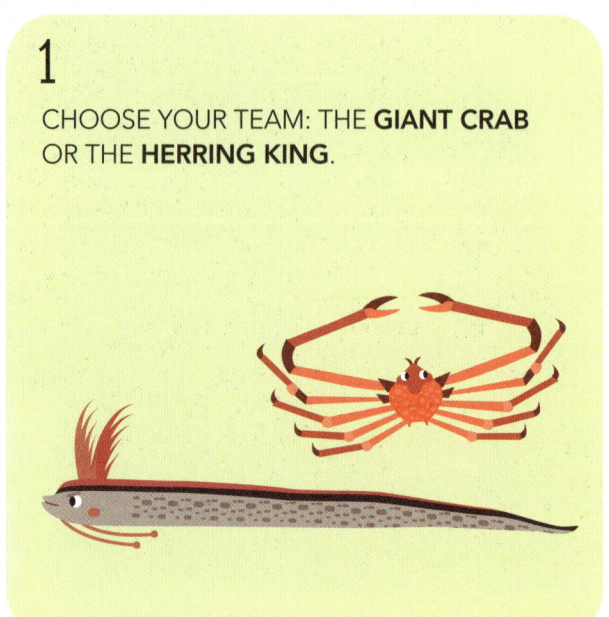

4

THE AIM OF THE GAME IS TO CONQUER THREE BASES BEFORE THE OTHER TEAM DOES. TO WIN A BASE, YOU MUST ATTACH AT LEAST THREE STICKERS.

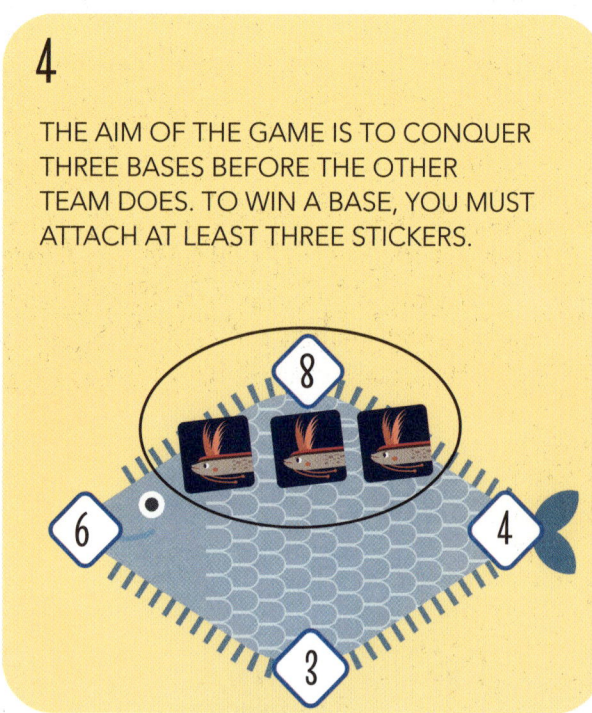

USE THIS PAGE AS THE GAME BOARD.

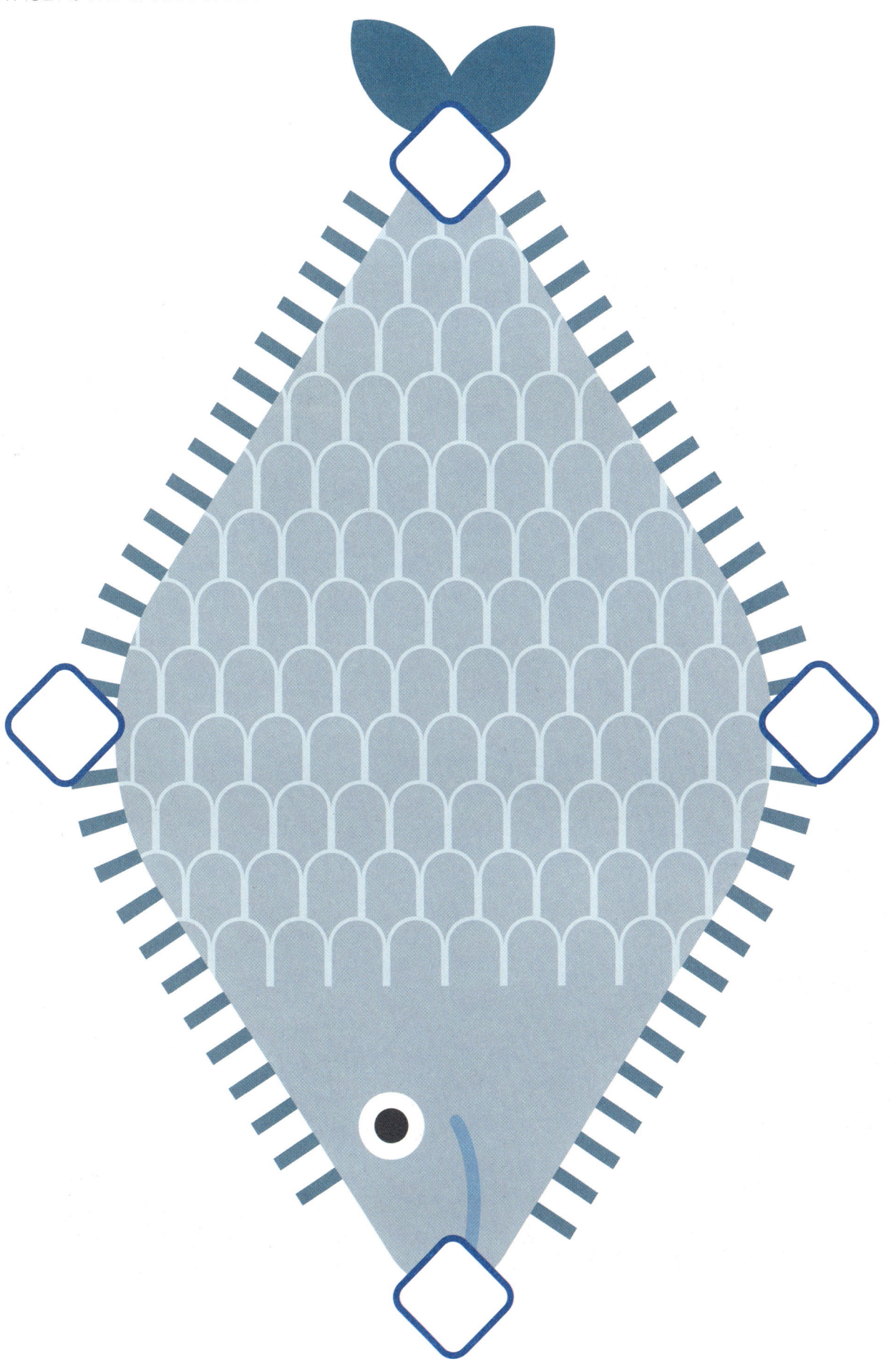

THE SUPREME COURT

ALTHOUGH MATH IS NOT AN OPINION, THE TWO TEAMS START FIGHTING ABOUT THE RESULTS. "WE WON!" "NO, WE DID!"
"WE'LL LET THE SUPREME COURT DECIDE WHO THE WINNER IS," PROPOSES THE HERRING KING, FLICKING HIS TAIL AS HE SWIMS BETWEEN THE PLAYERS. HELP THE JURORS FIND THEIR FLAGS. **SOLVE THE PROBLEMS** AND FIND THE FLAG **STICKER** WITH THE CORRECT NUMBER.

THE ESCAPE

WHILE THE JURORS DISCUSS THEIR VERDICT AND THE TEAMS SHOUT AMONG THEMSELVES, OLLY GOES OVER TO ASTER AND SAYS, **"IT'S TIME TO ESCAPE. WE HAVE TO GET BACK TO BOB!"** HELP THE TWO FRIENDS GET OUT OF THE ABYSS, FOLLOWING THE PATH WITH **MULTIPLES OF 7**.

THE CITY OF THE SCUBA DIVERS

"Hurry up! Over here!" calls Bob. "Before they realize we're gone."
Aster and Olly don't have to be told twice, and they quickly follow him to hide among some rocks. "I think the black bubbles are coming from the other side of these big rocks," murmurs the rockfish.
Olly looks around, perplexed. "Where are we?"
"Do these rocks look strange to you?" asks Aster, as she moves an anemone's tentacles to reveal an odd-looking shape.
"What a bizarre animal," comments Bob. "I've never seen anything like it."
"Yes, you have!" exclaims Olly.
"No, I haven't."
"You have! It's one of those bipedal animals with fins and a snorkel...What are they called? Ah! A scuba diver. I bet that's what it is."
"But it doesn't have fins," Bob points out.
"Or a snorkel," adds Aster.
"Maybe it's too young or too old to have them...Noooo! I know where we are. We're in the lost city of the Scuba Divers."
Olly is so excited that...PFFT! A cloud of ink squirts all over them.
"OLLY!"
"Sorry, I couldn't help myself. Do you realize where we are? This is Atlantis!"

THE SECRET PASSAGE

"PLATY, ONE OF THE SCUBA DIVERS' ANCIENT WISEMEN, SAID THAT THE CITY OF ATLANTIS WAS SUNK BY THE GOD OF THE SEA..." AS OLLY LISTENS TO THE STORY, HE LEANS ONE OF HIS TENTACLES AGAINST A ROCK. THE ROCKS START GROANING, THE WATER STARTS SHAKING, AND A **SECRET PASSAGE** APPEARS. CAN YOU FIND **WHERE OLLY PUT HIS TENTACLE?** THERE IS ONLY ONE CORRECT ANSWER!

A MAZE OF RUINS

"OOH, COME ON, LET'S GO INSIDE!" SAYS BOB ENTHUSIASTICALLY, PUSHING THEM TOWARD THE DARK OPENING. AS SOON AS THEY ARE INSIDE, THE DOOR CLOSES BEHIND THEM. "UMM...I'M NOT SURE THIS WAS A GOOD IDEA. IT'S A MAZE OF RUINS!" HELP ASTER, BOB, AND OLLY FIND THEIR WAY OUT: **COMPLETE THE PROBLEMS TO FIND THE RIGHT PATH.**

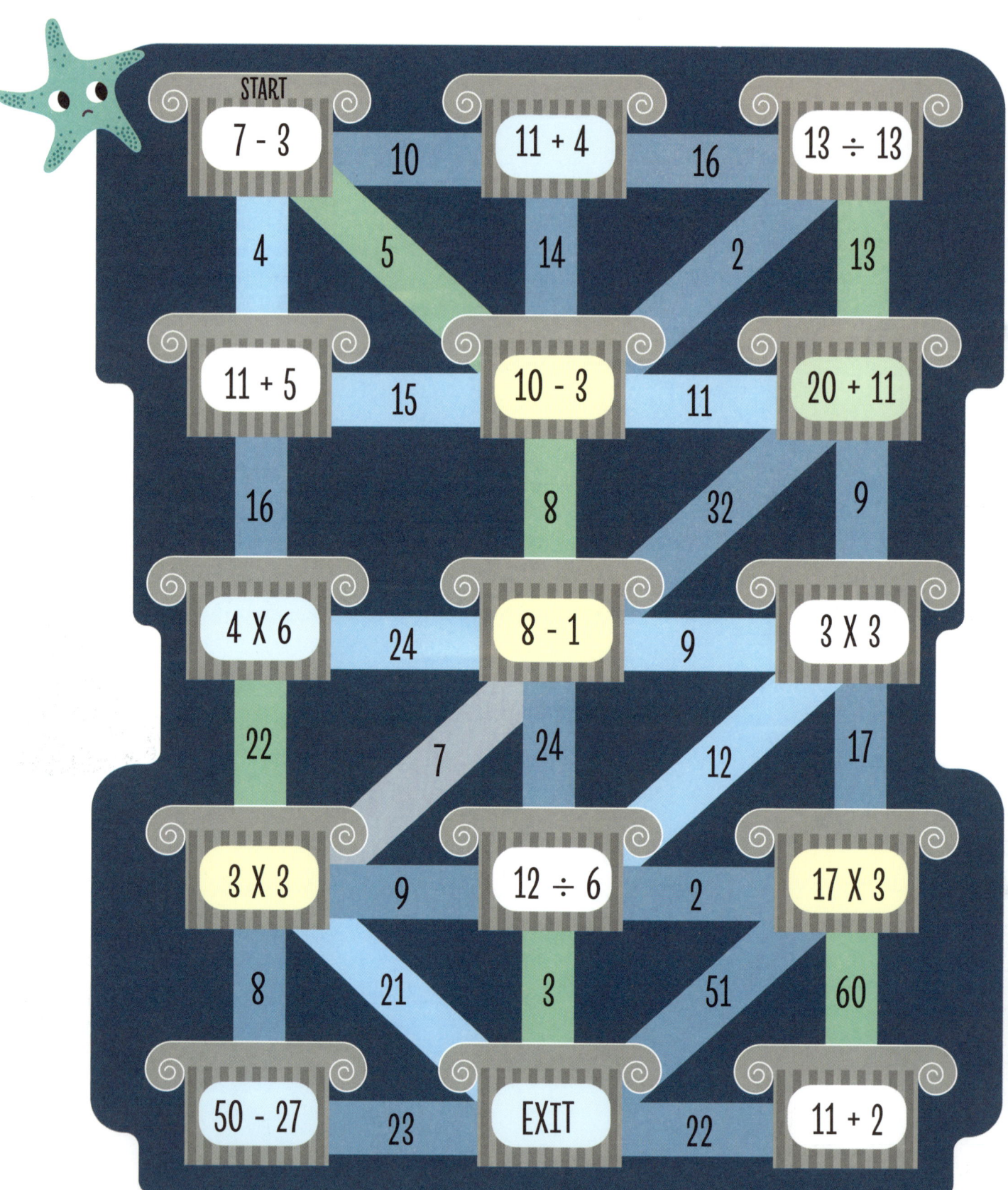

SPLOTCHES IN THE SQUARE

ASTER, BOB, AND OLLY FIND THEMSELVES IN ATLANTIS'S MAIN SQUARE, WHICH IS DECORATED FOR A PARTY. BUT THE INHABITANTS OF THE ANCIENT CITY LOOK VERY SAD. "WE WERE GOING TO HAVE A TIMES TABLE PARTY TODAY, WITH GAMES AND DANCES," GRUMBLES A HERMIT CRAB, "BUT THE BLACK BUBBLES HAVE DESTROYED EVERYTHING." "DON'T WORRY! WE'LL HELP YOU!"

SOLVE THE PROBLEMS ON THE BUBBLES, FIND THE RIGHT SHELL STICKER, AND STOP THE BUBBLES FROM DOING ANY MORE DAMAGE.

LET'S REPAIR THE BANNERS

THE BUBBLES SEEM TO HAVE STOPPED CAUSING HAVOC, BUT THE DAMAGE NEEDS TO BE REPAIRED. **THE BUBBLES HAVE ERASED SOME OF THE NUMBERS ON THE BANNERS.** CAN YOU WORK OUT WHAT THEY WERE?

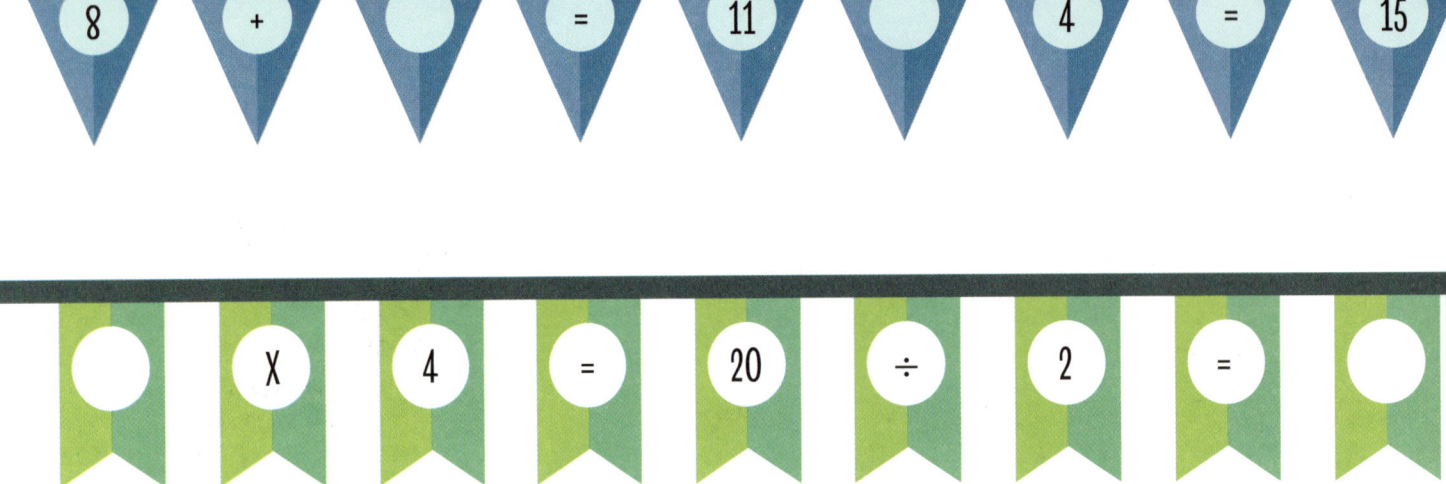

CRYPTIC CHOREOGRAPHIES

THE TERRIFIED CRABS AND JELLYFISH HAVE FORGOTTEN THEIR NUMERICAL CHOREOGRAPHIES. HELP THEM REMEMBER BY COMPLETING THE TABLES WITH THE CORRECT **STICKERS**. USE THE EXAMPLES TO HELP YOU.

34

COUNT THE MISSING SEA CREATURES

SOME OF THE PARTICIPANTS ARE MISSING. SOLVE THE PROBLEMS TO FIND OUT WHO IS MISSING, AND THEN ATTACH THE **STICKER** WITH THE CORRECT NUMBER OF SEA CREATURES ON IT.

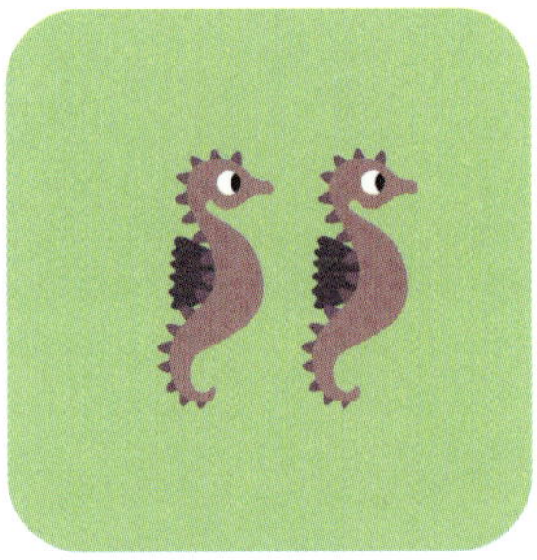

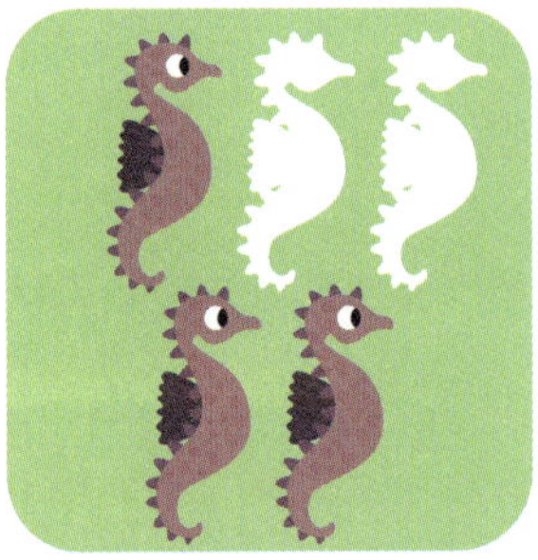

 = 10   HOW MANY ARE MISSING?

 = 11   HOW MANY ARE MISSING?

 = 16   HOW MANY ARE MISSING?

 = 9   HOW MANY ARE MISSING?

THE MYSTERY OF KING PLAICE

WITH EVERYONE LENDING A HAND, ASTER, BOB, OLLY, AND THE SEA CREATURES OF ATLANTIS MANAGE TO REPAIR ALL OF THE DAMAGE CAUSED BY THE BUBBLES.
THE CITY REJOICES AND STARTS CELEBRATING. "THE BUBBLES ARE COMING FROM SOMEWHERE NEAR HERE," EXPLAINS KING PLAICE, THE CITY'S RULER. "IF YOU SOLVE THE MYSTERY, THE ENTIRE OCEAN WILL BE IN YOUR DEBT. WE'LL TELL YOU HOW TO GET OUT, SO YOU CAN CONTINUE YOUR JOURNEY."

SOLVE THE PROBLEMS IN THE SQUARES AND COMPLETE THE PARTY WITH THE STICKERS.

9 - 6

15 - 8

52 ÷ 4

12 - 6

18 ÷ 9

10 ÷ 10

35 ÷ 7

33 ÷ 3

8 X 2

123 - 113

7 X 2

7 X 2

THE LOST CEMETERY

After walking a bit and then swimming for a while, the three friends finally emerge from the ruins. The stream of black bubbles has become so thick that it's really difficult to dodge them.

"King Plaice was right," shouts Olly, darting right, then left, then right again, then down to avoid all the bubbles. "We're almost there!"

Bob gasps. "Look at those strange shapes over there. What are they?"

"I think they're shipwrecks," replies Aster, rising from the sand to speak.

"Ships? Those huge, noisy shells that scuba divers move around in?"

"Exactly," replies the starfish. "I accidentally interrupted a conversation between some sea urchins. They said that there's loads of food around those ships over there."

"Wait a minute...," say Bob and Olly, stopping suddenly in their tracks and turning to stare at her. "What do you mean by you 'interrupted a conversation'?"

"Well," says Aster, with an angelic smile, "I kind of had a nibble..."

"Aster, you're incorrigible!" exclaim Bob and Olly indignantly. The three friends set off across the part sandy, part rocky ocean floor toward the huge silhouettes of the shipwrecks.

THE PATH BETWEEN THE BUBBLES

THE THREE FRIENDS FIND THEMSELVES IN FRONT OF **A WALL OF BLACK BUBBLES**. OLLY HAS DECIDED THAT HE WILL GUIDE THEM OUT OF DANGER. HELP HIM FIND THE RIGHT WAY. ANSWER THE QUESTIONS COLUMN BY COLUMN, AND ATTACH THE STICKERS ON THE CORRECT NUMBERS TO OPEN THE **PATH BETWEEN THE BUBBLES**.

SUBTRACT 12 TO GET 5	IT'S DIVISIBLE BY 3	IT'S DIVISIBLE BY 4	ADD 3 TO GET 7	IT'S DIVISIBLE BY 5	IT'S DIVISIBLE BY 2	MULTIPLY BY 9 TO GET 54
13	5	16	4	15	11	8
21	9	32	3	10	4	7
17	6	9	2	7	8	5
19	2	15	1	11	12	6

START

EXIT

THE STEEP CLIMB

A GIANT SHIP SUDDENLY APPEARS IN FRONT OF THEM.
"THE BUBBLES APPEAR TO BE COMING FROM THAT **HOLE**."
"COME ON! LET'S FIND OUT WHAT'S MAKING THEM."
BUT GETTING UP THERE ISN'T GOING TO BE EASY...

11 + 18 =

57 - 36 =

18 X 3 =

66 -
25 =

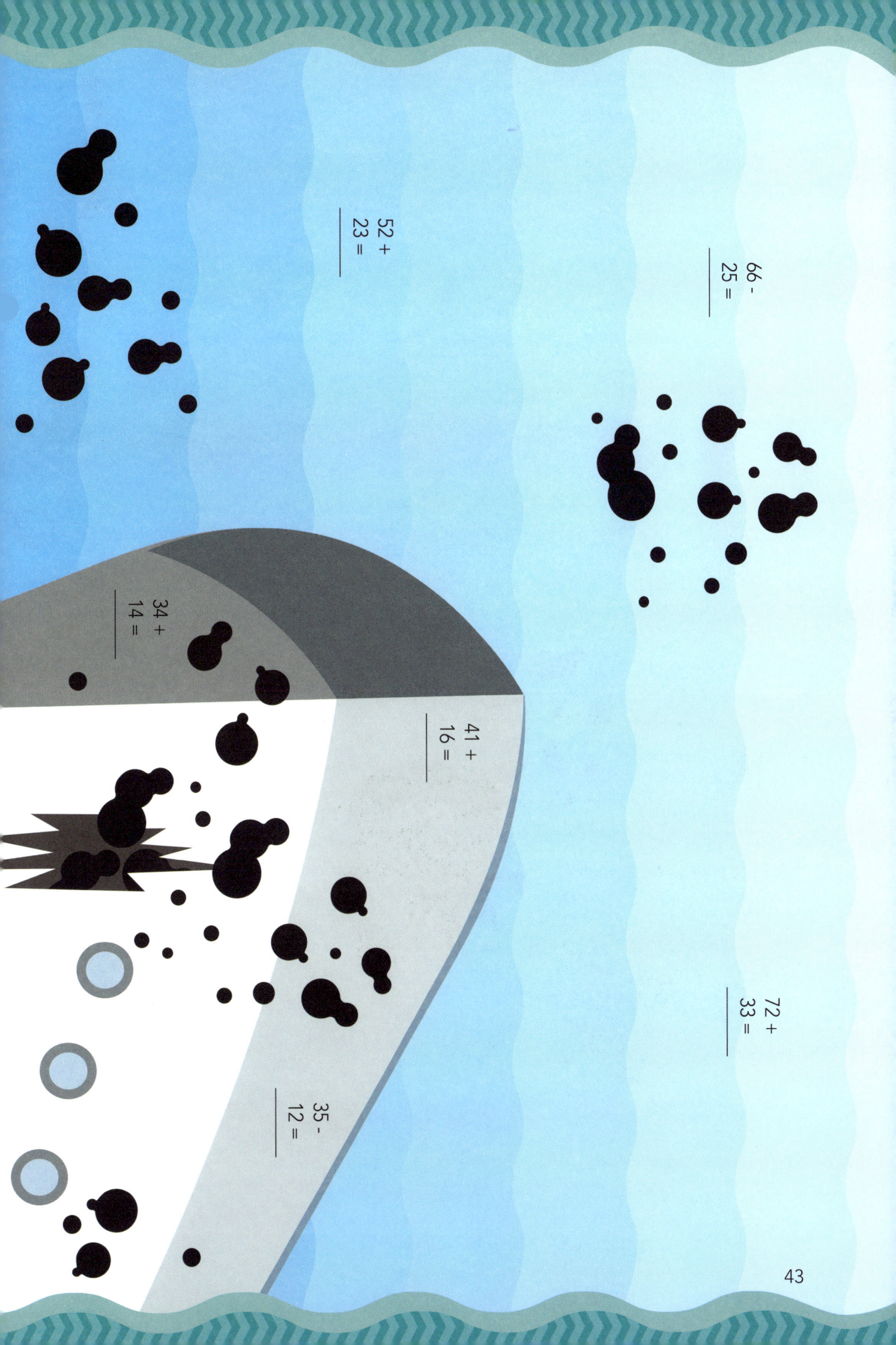

52 +
23 =

34 +
14 =

41 +
16 =

72 +
33 =

35 -
12 =

SMACK!
THE THREE FRIENDS PEER DOWN THE HOLE.
"OH NOOOO!!!" CRY BOB AND ASTER AS A HUGE BUBBLE HITS OLLY IN THE FACE...
THEY BOTH FREEZE.
"HEY! YOU HAVEN'T BEEN ERASED."
"IT DOESN'T SEEM LIKE IT...I'M STILL HERE. AND I FEEL FINE."
"ARE YOU SURE?"
"YES."
"ABSOLUTELY SURE? YOU DON'T FEEL..."
"I'M FINE! IT'S JUST...**INK**."
ASTER AND BOB WATCH OLLY WORRIEDLY AS HE EXAMINES HIS TENTACLES, BUT HE'S STILL THERE, ALIVE AND WELL. THE THREE FRIENDS GO BACK TO THE HOLE IN THE WRECK. SUDDENLY, SOME LIGHTS APPEAR IN THE DARKNESS...

COMPLETE THE PROBLEMS AND CONNECT THE DOTS IN THE ORDER OF THE ANSWERS TO FIND OUT WHO, OR WHAT, THE LIGHTS BELONG TO.

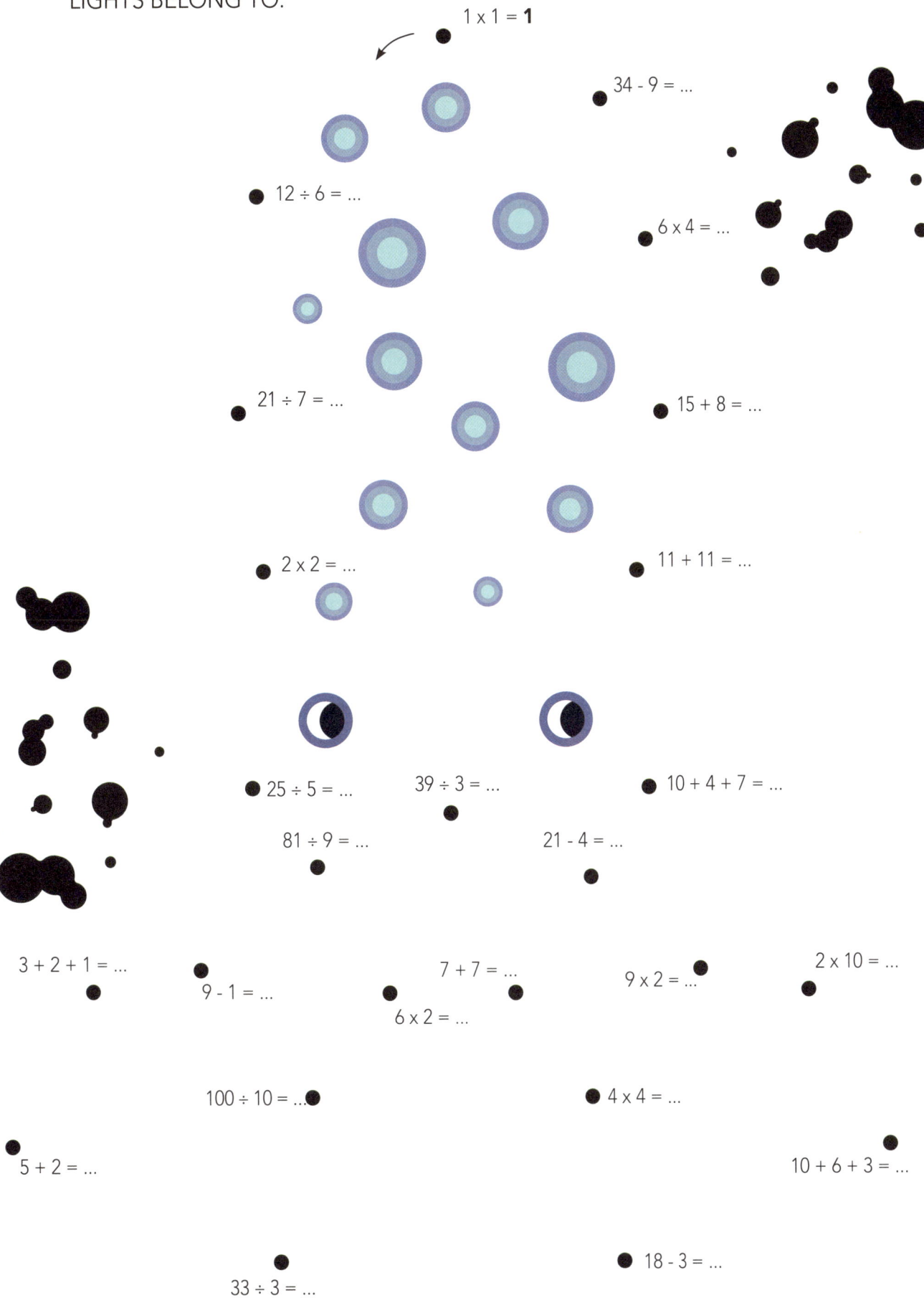

1 x 1 = **1**

34 - 9 = ...

12 ÷ 6 = ...

6 x 4 = ...

21 ÷ 7 = ...

15 + 8 = ...

2 x 2 = ...

11 + 11 = ...

25 ÷ 5 = ...   39 ÷ 3 = ...   10 + 4 + 7 = ...

81 ÷ 9 = ...   21 - 4 = ...

3 + 2 + 1 = ...   7 + 7 = ...   9 x 2 = ...   2 x 10 = ...
           9 - 1 = ...   6 x 2 = ...

100 ÷ 10 = ...   4 x 4 = ...

5 + 2 = ...   10 + 6 + 3 = ...

18 - 3 = ...

33 ÷ 3 = ...

45

ANGRY SQUID

A HUGE SQUID EMERGES FROM THE SHADOWS, FOLLOWED BY ANOTHER, AND ANOTHER, UNTIL THE SHIP'S DARK HOLD IS FILLED WITH COLORFUL LIGHTS.
"HELLO," SAYS BOB, NERVOUSLY.
"IS THAT ALL YOU HAVE TO SAY?" ASKS THE ANGRY CEPHALOPOD NEAREST TO THEM.
"WE'VE BEEN DOWN HERE TRYING TO SOLVE THESE PROBLEMS FOR DAYS! ARGH!!"
"ARGH!!" ALL THE OTHER SQUID REPEAT IN CHORUS. MEANWHILE, A NEW STREAM OF BLACK BUBBLES STARTS FORMING BETWEEN THEIR TENTACLES.

"**THEY'RE THE ONES MAKING THE BUBBLES!**" WHISPERS ASTER.
"STOP! DON'T GET UPSET," SAYS OLLY IN A REASSURING VOICE. "WE CAN HELP YOU... I THINK."
ANGRY SQUID ARE MAKING THE BUBBLES. HELP THEM CALM DOWN BY SOLVING THE PROBLEMS. HERE'S THE **FIRST TABLET**: THERE ARE SOME **ADDITION PROBLEMS** HIDDEN IN THE NUMBER GRID. CAN YOU FIND THEM? LOOK FOR THEM BOTH **HORIZONTALLY** AND **VERTICALLY**, COMPLETE THEM WITH THE **+** AND **=** SIGNS, AND THEN CIRCLE THEM AS SHOWN IN THE EXAMPLES.

0	2	3	5	4	3	8	0
6	3	4	0	1	5	2	7
0	6	3	9	3	4	2	8
4	7	1	5	4	9	1	0
1	2	4	3	3	2	6	8
6	4	0	6	4	3	7	1
7	2	9	2	1	8	4	5
3	3	6	2	8	1	9	0
0	5	4	4	8	7	2	5

MARINE PROBLEMS

ASTER, BOB, AND OLLY CONCENTRATE ON SOLVING THE SQUID'S EXERCISES. "IF YOU'D BEEN HERE TO HELP US, WE'D NEVER HAVE GOTTEN SO ANGRY!" COMMENTS ONE OF THE SQUID ADMIRINGLY. "AND WE WOULDN'T HAVE GOTTEN SO MANY VILE BUBBLES!" ADDS OLLY, LAUGHING.

THE **SECOND TABLET** CONTAINS **MARINE PROBLEMS**: READ THEM CAREFULLY AND FIND THE ANSWERS.

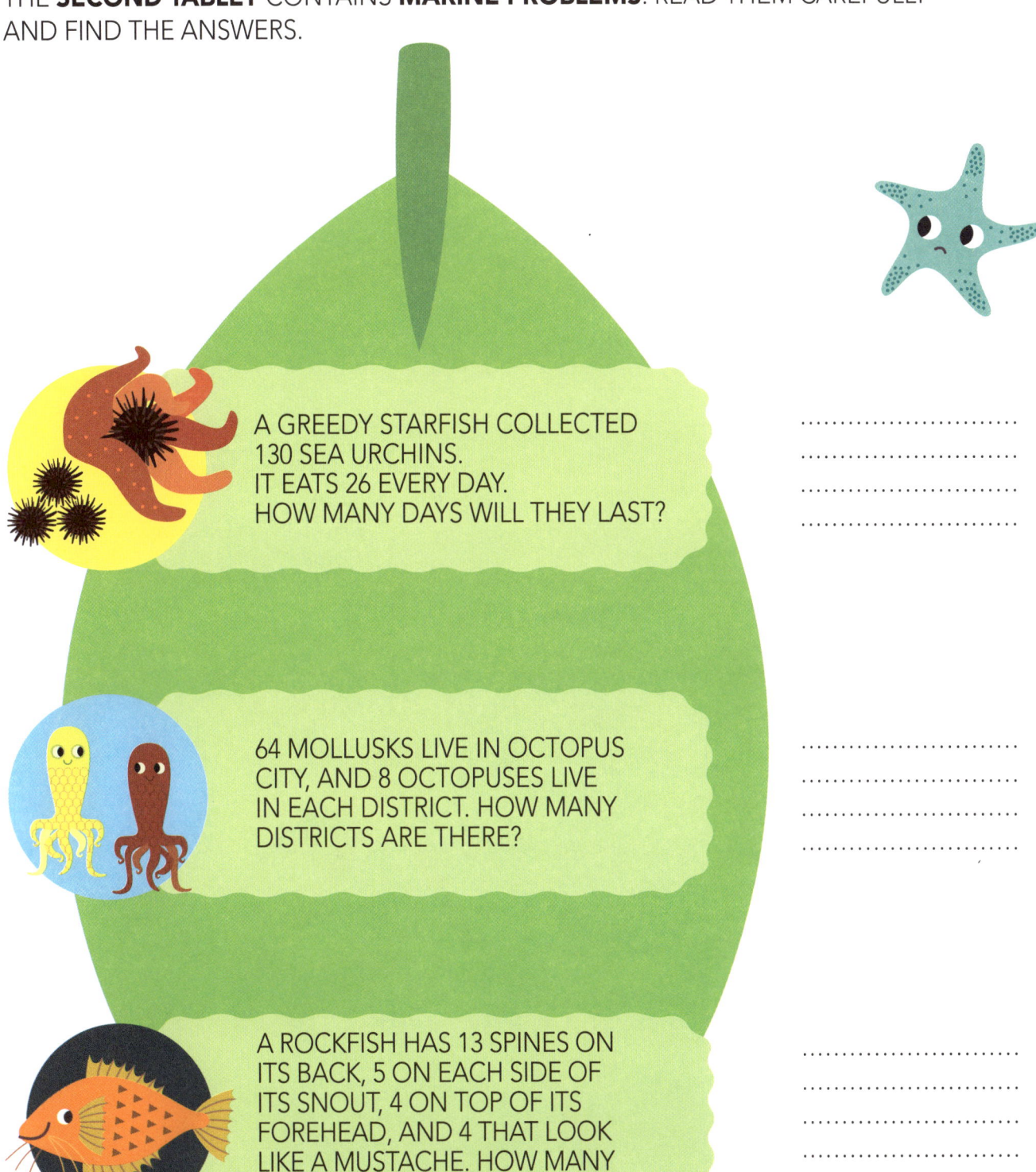

A GREEDY STARFISH COLLECTED 130 SEA URCHINS.
IT EATS 26 EVERY DAY.
HOW MANY DAYS WILL THEY LAST?

64 MOLLUSKS LIVE IN OCTOPUS CITY, AND 8 OCTOPUSES LIVE IN EACH DISTRICT. HOW MANY DISTRICTS ARE THERE?

A ROCKFISH HAS 13 SPINES ON ITS BACK, 5 ON EACH SIDE OF ITS SNOUT, 4 ON TOP OF ITS FOREHEAD, AND 4 THAT LOOK LIKE A MUSTACHE. HOW MANY SPINES DOES IT HAVE IN TOTAL?

THE PROPHECY

"WHY ARE YOU SO INTERESTED IN THESE STRANGE TABLETS WITH EXERCISES ON THEM?" ASKS BOB. "THEY'RE THE TABLETS OF THE **MATH PROPHECY**!" EXPLAINS ONE OF THE SQUID. "CENTURIES AGO, THE GREAT MOLLUSK SAID THEY WOULD LEAD US TO **GREAT VALLEYS** WITHOUT ANY PREDATORS. THE SECRET IS FINDING THE PROBLEMS TO WHICH THE ANSWER IS **EIGHT**."

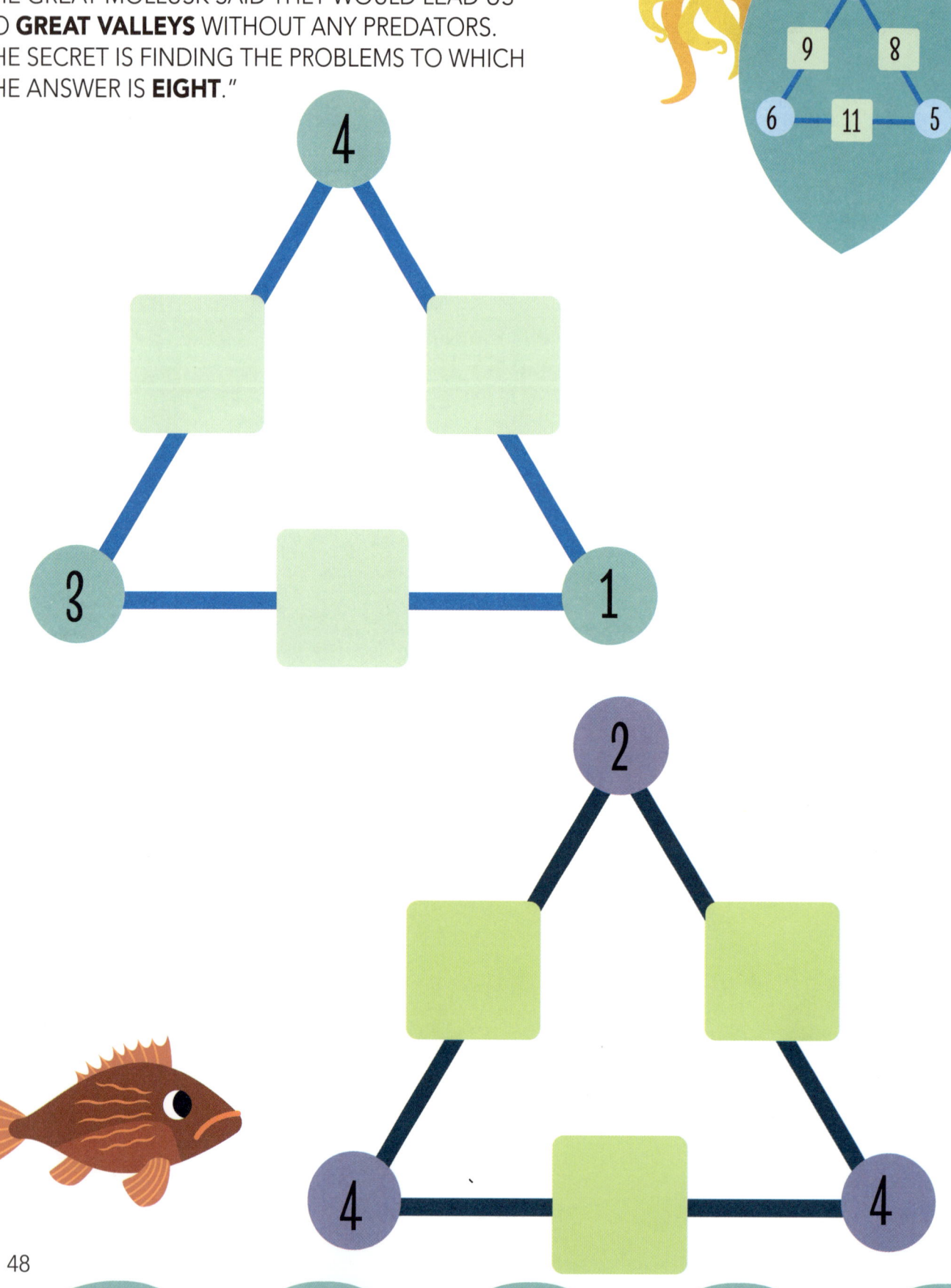

COMPLETE THE MATHEMATICAL INSCRIPTIONS WITH THE STICKERS. **THE NUMBERS IN THE SQUARES ARE THE SUM OF THE NUMBERS IN THE CIRCLES THEY ARE CONNECTED TO.** USE OLLY'S EXAMPLE TO HELP YOU.

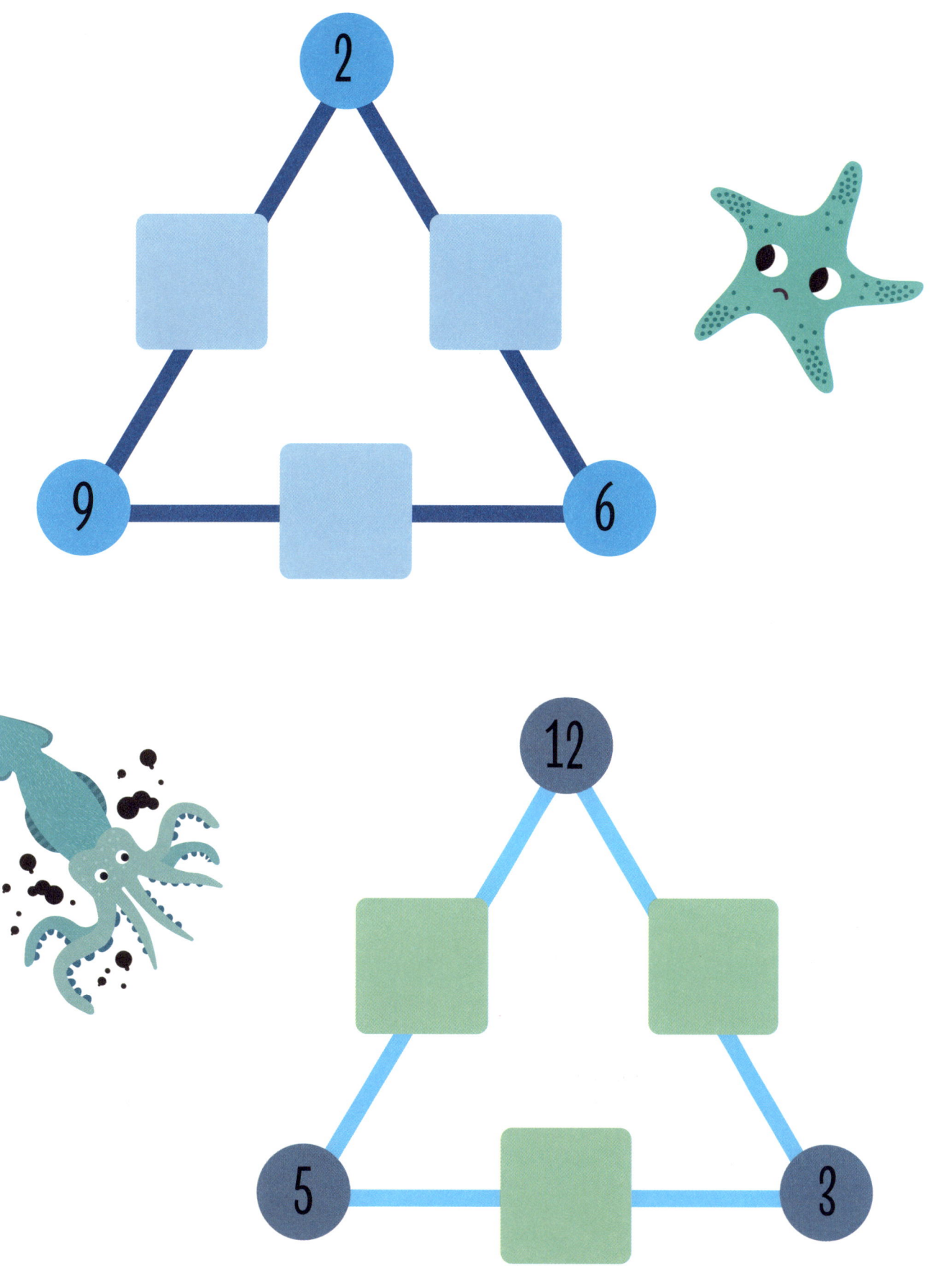

THE FINAL TEST

WE'RE ALMOST THERE. THE FINISH LINE IS IN SIGHT!
BUT BEFORE THEY GET THERE, BOB, OLLY, AND ASTER HAVE TO CROSS SOME VERY **DANGEROUS WATERS**. HELP THEM PASS SAFELY BETWEEN THE SHARKS, JELLYFISH, AND WHIRLPOOLS. FOLLOW THE ARROWS AND **ATTACH THE NUMBER OF STICKERS INDICATED BY THE WHITE NUMBERS**. BUT BEWARE: YOU MUST ALSO STICK THEM ON THE ARROWS!

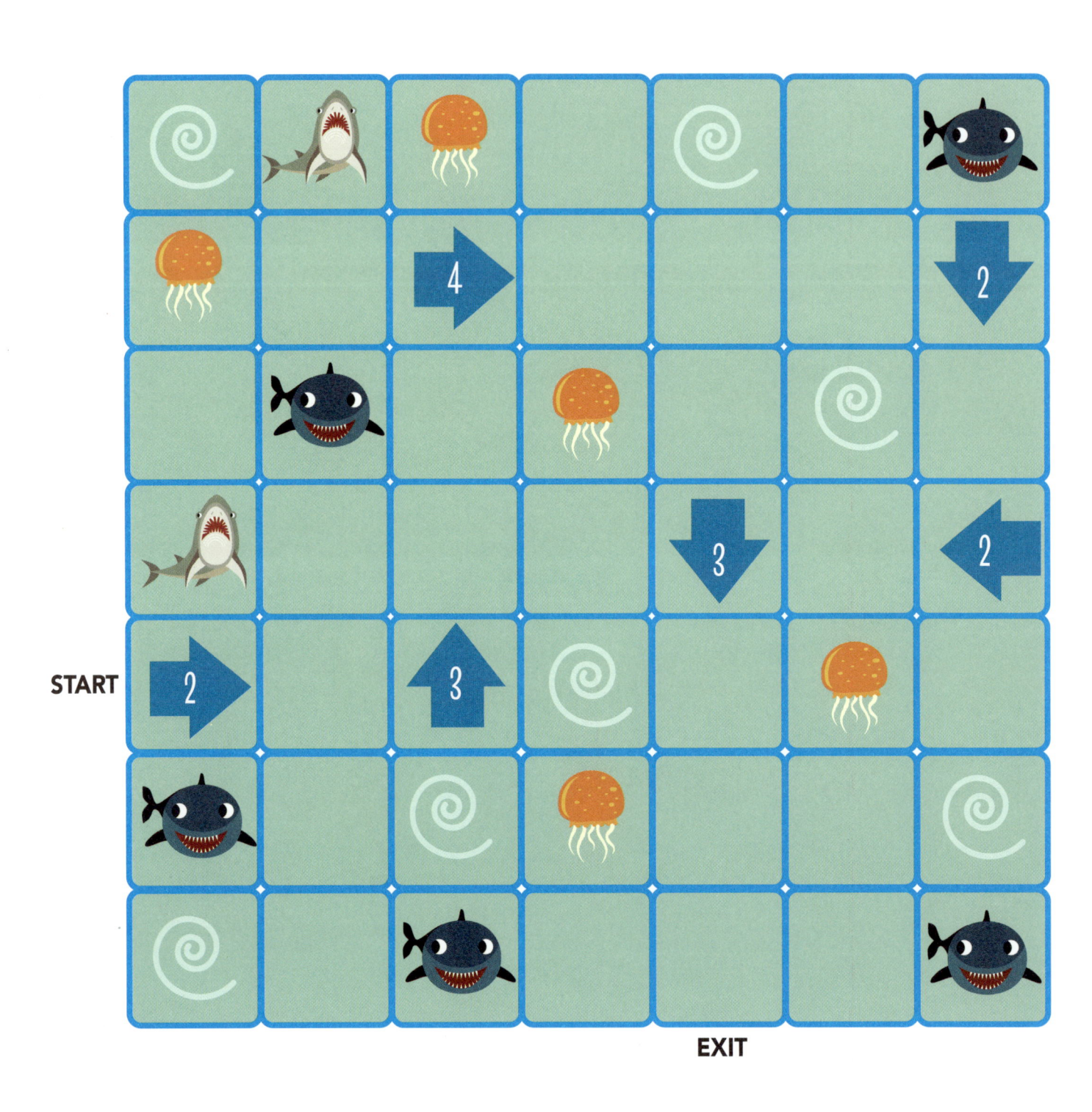

START

EXIT

CONGRATULATIONS!

THANKS TO YOU, ASTER, BOB, AND OLLY, THE SQUID HAVE FOUND ALL THE PROBLEMS THAT EQUAL **8**, AND THEY'VE FINALLY BEEN ABLE TO DECODE THE MATH PROPHECY. ATTACH THE CORRECT **STICKERS** AND FIND OUT WHERE **SHRIMP PARADISE** IS.

- $+ 6 = 8$
- $\div 2 = 8$
- $+ 5 = 8$
- $+ 2 = 8$
- $\div 8 = 8$
- $+ 4 = 8$
- $+ 3 = 8$
- $\div 3 = 8$

SHRIMP PARADISE

DECIMAL RIDGE

GREAT VALLEY

NOW THAT THE BLACK BUBBLES HAVE GONE AWAY, AND THE OCEAN IS CALM AGAIN, THE THREE FRIENDS CAN FINALLY GO HOME.
"BOB, I KNOW WHAT I WANT TO BE WHEN I GROW UP... A MATH TEACHER!"
"THAT'S GREAT, OLLY! I WANT TO BE A GARDENER, SO I CAN CARRY ON CARING FOR MY ROCK. WHAT ABOUT YOU, ASTER?...ASTER? WHERE...?"

ANSWERS

P. 5 LET'S GET SUPPLIES!

4 X 3 = 12
6 X 2 = 12
2 X 3 = 6
8 + 3 = 11
8 ÷ 8 = 1
14 - 2 = 12
3 + 9 = 12
6 + 7 = 13
8 + 4 = 12
7 - 2 = 5
9 - 2 = 7
12 ÷ 1 = 12
6 + 6 = 12
10 + 2 = 12
6 + 5 = 11
5 X 3 = 15
10 - 2 = 8
2 X 7 = 14
20 - 8 = 12
2 X 5 = 10
5 + 7 = 12
2 + 8 = 10
1 + 11 = 12

PP. 6–7 WHICH WAY SHALL WE GO?

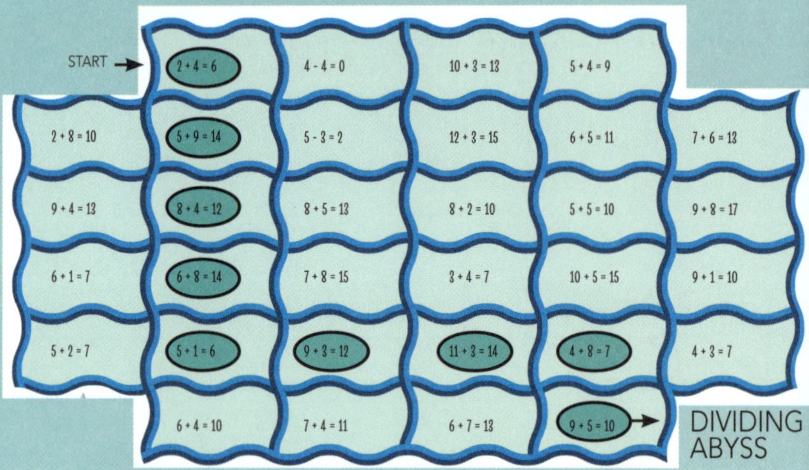
START
2 + 4 = 6
4 - 4 = 0
10 + 3 = 13
5 + 4 = 9
2 + 8 = 10
5 + 9 = 14
5 - 3 = 2
12 + 3 = 15
6 + 5 = 11
7 + 6 = 13
9 + 4 = 13
8 + 4 = 12
8 + 5 = 13
8 + 2 = 10
5 + 5 = 10
9 + 8 = 17
6 + 1 = 7
6 + 8 = 14
7 + 8 = 15
3 + 4 = 7
10 + 5 = 15
9 + 1 = 10
5 + 2 = 7
5 + 1 = 6
9 + 3 = 12
11 + 3 = 14
4 + 8 = 7
4 + 3 = 7
6 + 4 = 10
7 + 4 = 11
6 + 7 = 13
9 + 5 = 10
DIVIDING ABYSS

P. 9 CLARA'S EGGS

7 + 3 = 10   5 + 4 = 9   6 + 2 = 8   3 + 4 = 7

P. 9 SPECIES ON THE CORAL REEF

SPECIES	SCENE 1	SCENE 2	SCENE 3	SCENE 4	TOTAL
	4	4	2	4	14
	3	2	4	3	12
	2	3	3	2	10
	2	1	3	2	8

P. 10 WHO BELONGS TO WHO?

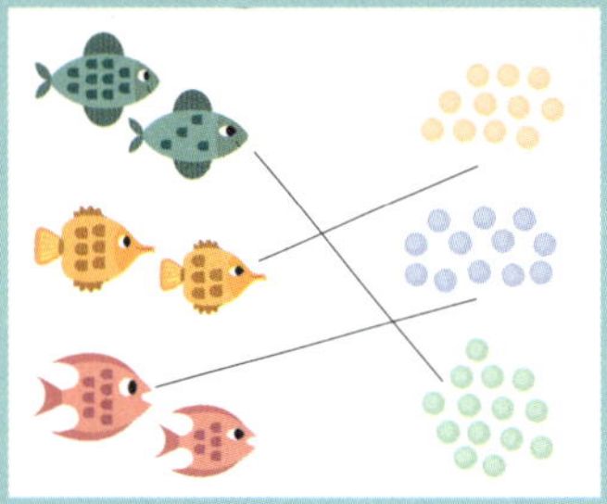

P. 11 A MULTICOLORED CORAL REEF

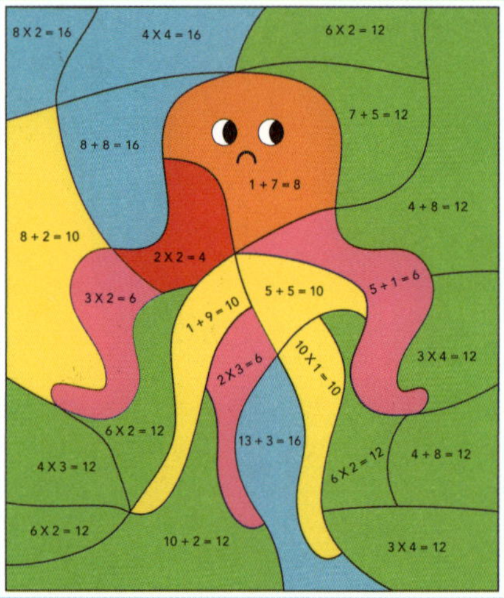
8 X 2 = 16
4 X 4 = 16
6 X 2 = 12
7 + 5 = 12
8 + 8 = 16
1 + 7 = 8
4 + 8 = 12
8 + 2 = 10
2 X 2 = 4
3 X 2 = 6
5 + 5 = 10
5 + 1 = 6
1 + 9 = 10
2 X 3 = 6
10 X 1 = 10
3 X 4 = 12
6 X 2 = 12
13 + 3 = 16
4 X 3 = 12
6 X 2 = 12
4 + 8 = 12
6 X 2 = 12
10 + 2 = 12
3 X 4 = 12

P. 12 PREDATORS AND PREY

9 - 3 = 6   6 - 4 = 2   7 - 5 = 2   8 - 1 = 7   9 - 7 = 2   5 - 4 = 1   8 - 6 = 2   7 - 1 = 6   8 - 2 = 6

P. 13 OTHER PREDATORS

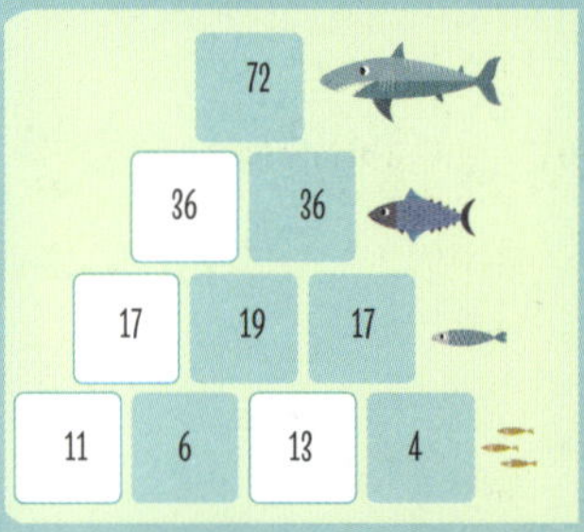
72
36
36
17
19
17
11
6
13
4

48
22
26
10
12
14
7
3
9
5

P. 14 LET'S REPAIR THE CORAL REEF

P. 15 THE JOURNEY CONTINUES

7
- 4
= 3
X 3
= 9
+ 2
11
+ 4
= 15
÷ 3
= 5
- 2
= 3

P. 16 THE EDGE OF THE CORAL REEF

ASTER 1 - 2 - 3 - 4 - 5 - 6 - 7 - 8 - 9 - 10 - 11 - 12 - 13 - 14 - 15 - 16
BOB 4 - 8 - 12 - 16
OLLY 2 - 4 - 6 - 8 - 10 - 12 - 14 - 16

P. 19 DIVING INTO THE ABYSS

PP. 20–21 FORM YOUR TEAMS

P. 22 LET THE FIRST CHALLENGE BEGIN!

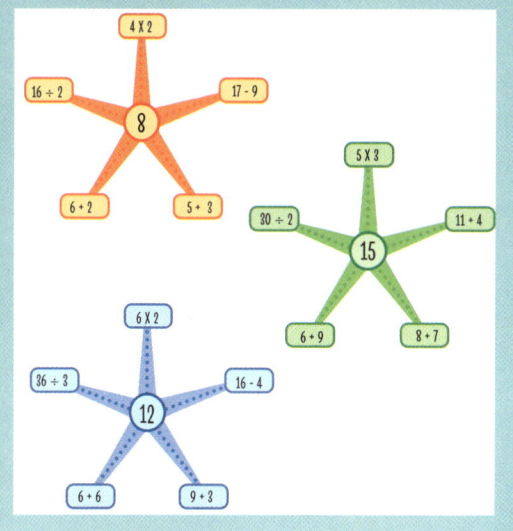

P. 23 THE REVERSE FISH CHALLENGE

PP. 24–25 THE SPERM WHALES

P. 28 THE SUPREME COURT

P. 29 THE ESCAPE!

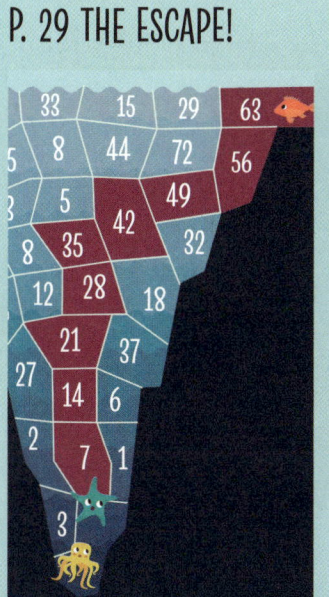

P. 31 THE SECRET PASSAGE

P. 32 A MAZE OF RUINS

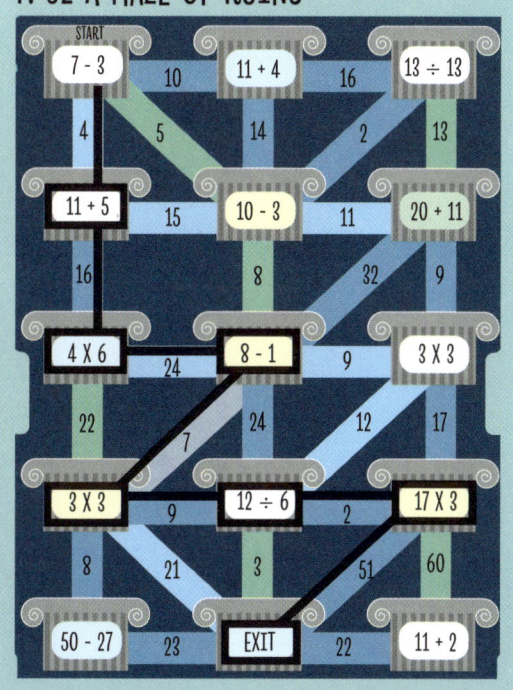

P. 33 SPLOTCHES IN THE SQUARE

5 X 5 = 25   36 ÷ 6 = 6   10 X 4 = 40   6 X 9 = 54

45 ÷ 9 = 5   81 ÷ 9 = 9   42 ÷ 6 = 7   32 ÷ 4 = 8

PP. 34–35 LET'S REPAIR THE BANNERS

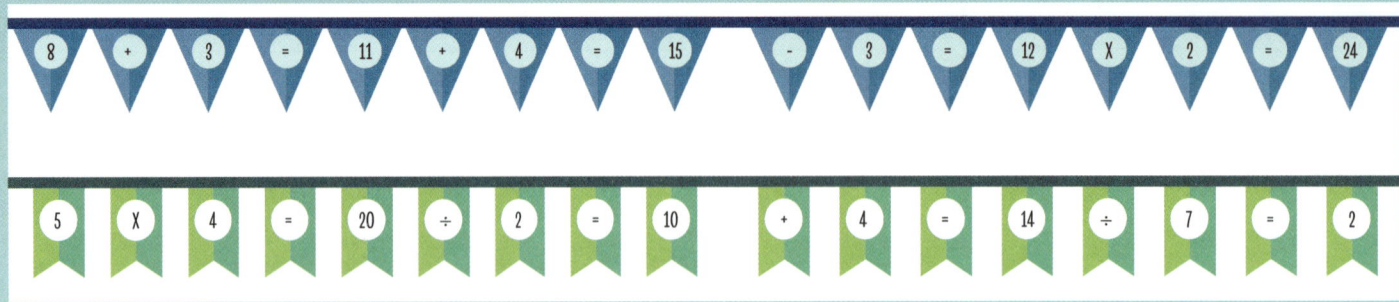

8 + 3 = 11 + 4 = 15 − 3 = 12 X 2 = 24

5 X 4 = 20 ÷ 2 = 10 + 4 = 14 ÷ 7 = 2

PP. 34–35 CRYPTIC CHOREOGRAPHIES

+	10	11	12
3	13	14	15
2	12	13	14
1	11	12	13

−	5	4	3
8	3	4	5
7	2	3	4
6	1	2	3

PP. 36–37 COUNT THE MISSING SEA CREATURES

HOW MANY ARE MISSING?

PP. 38–39 THE MYSTERY OF KING PLAICE

18 ÷ 9 = 2
10 ÷ 10 = 1
9 − 6 = 3
35 ÷ 7 = 5
33 ÷ 3 = 11
8 X 2 = 16
123 − 113 = 10
7 X 2 = 14
52 ÷ 4 = 13
15 − 8 = 7
12 − 6 = 6
7 X 2 = 14

P. 41 THE PATH BETWEEN THE BUBBLES

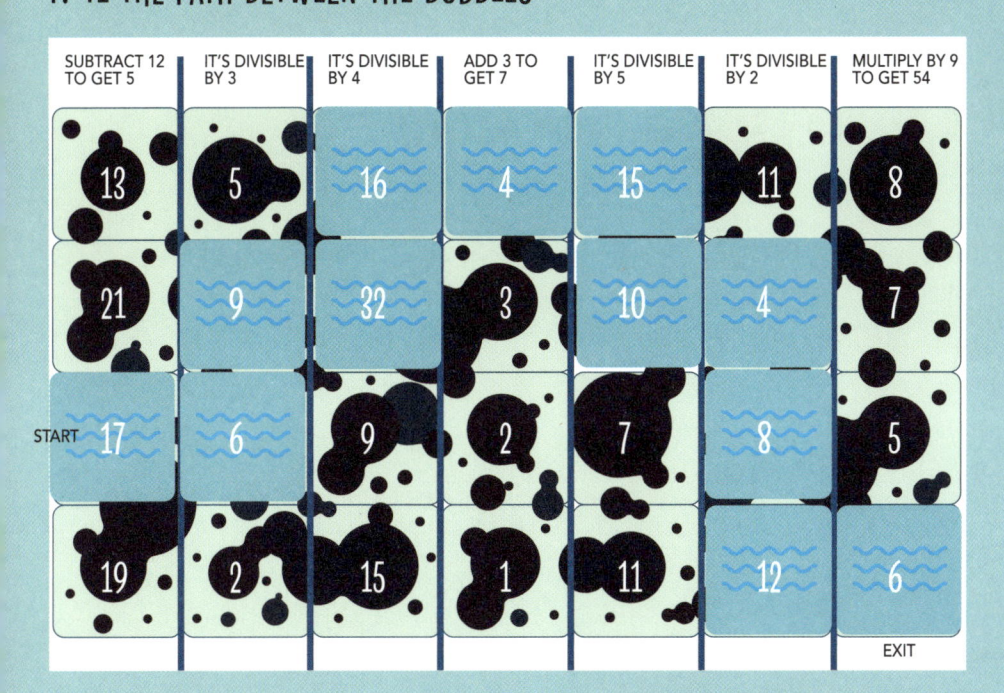

SUBTRACT 12 TO GET 5	IT'S DIVISIBLE BY 3	IT'S DIVISIBLE BY 4	ADD 3 TO GET 7	IT'S DIVISIBLE BY 5	IT'S DIVISIBLE BY 2	MULTIPLY BY 9 TO GET 54
13	5	16	4	15	11	8
21	9	32	3	10	4	7
START 17	6	9	2	7	8	5
19	2	15	1	11	12	6 EXIT

PP. 42–43 THE STEEP CLIMB

$52 + 23 = 75$

$34 + 14 = 48$

$66 - 25 = 41$

$11 + 18 = 29$

$41 + 16 = 57$

$57 - 36 = 21$

$18 \times 3 = 54$

$35 - 12 = 23$

$72 + 33 = 105$

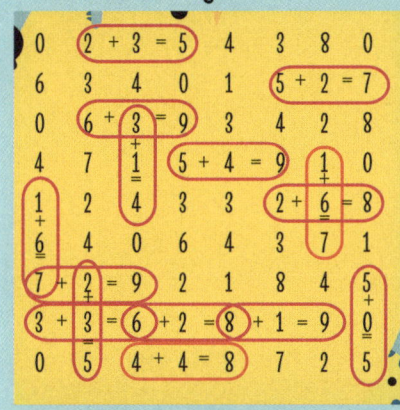

P. 47 MARINE PROBLEMS

THE GREEDY STARFISH
$130 \div 26 = 5$

OCTOPUS CITY
$64 \div 8 = 8$

THE ROCKFISH'S SPINES
$13 + (5 \times 2) + 4 + 4 = 31$

P. 45 SMACK!

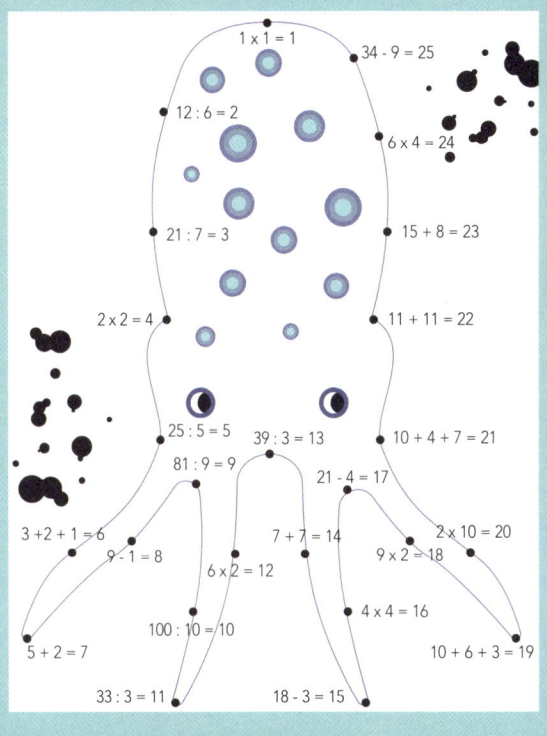

$1 \times 1 = 1$
$34 - 9 = 25$
$12 : 6 = 2$
$6 \times 4 = 24$
$21 : 7 = 3$
$15 + 8 = 23$
$2 \times 2 = 4$
$11 + 11 = 22$
$25 : 5 = 5$
$39 : 3 = 13$
$10 + 4 + 7 = 21$
$81 : 9 = 9$
$21 - 4 = 17$
$3 + 2 + 1 = 6$
$2 \times 10 = 20$
$9 - 1 = 8$
$7 + 7 = 14$
$9 \times 2 = 18$
$6 \times 2 = 12$
$4 \times 4 = 16$
$100 : 10 = 10$
$10 + 6 + 3 = 19$
$5 + 2 = 7$
$33 : 3 = 11$
$18 - 3 = 15$

P. 46 ANGRY SQUID

0	2	+	3	=	5	4	3	8	0
6	3	4	0	1	5	+	2	=	7
0	6	+	3	=	9	3	4	2	8
4	7	1	5	+	4	=	9	1	0
		+						+	
1	2	4	3	3	3	2	+	6	= 8
+									
6	8	4	0	6	4	3	7	1	
7	+	2	=	9	2	1	8	4	5 +
3	+	3	=	6	+	2	=	8	+	1	= 9	0 =
0	5	4	+	4	=	8	7	2	5

PP. 48–49 THE PROPHECY

Triangle 1: 4 (top), 7, 5, 3, 4, 1
Triangle 2: 12 (top), 17, 15, 5, 8, 3
Triangle 3: 2 (top), 11, 8, 9, 15, 6
Triangle 4: 2 (top), 6, 6, 4, 8, 4

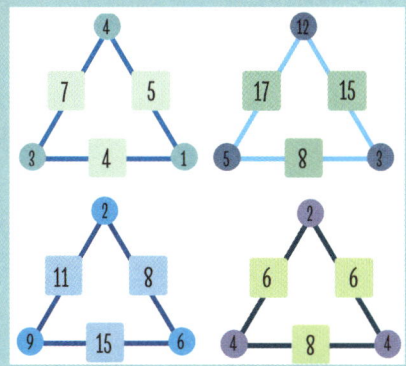

P. 50 THE FINAL TEST

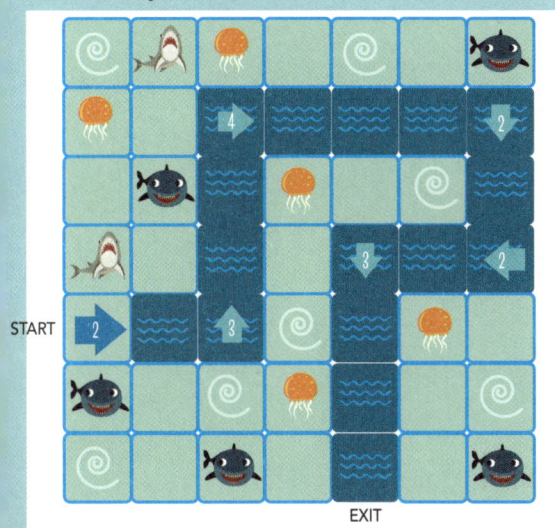

P. 51 CONGRATULATIONS!

$2 + 6 = 8$
$16 \div 2 = 8$
$3 + 5 = 8$
$6 + 2 = 8$
$64 \div 8 = 8$
$4 + 4 = 8$
$5 + 3 = 8$
$24 \div 3 = 8$

TECNOSCIENZA

Tecnoscienza is a group of authors and educators who for more than 15 years have been involved in the dissemination of science, technology, mathematics, and information about the environment for numerous institutions, such as museums and businesses. Their books have been published in more than 20 countries and are designed to stimulate thoughts, actions, and emotions.

AGNESE BARUZZI

Agnese has a degree in graphic design from ISIA (Institute of Higher Education in the Artistic Industries) in Urbino, Italy. Since 2001, she has been working as an illustrator and author; she has created numerous children's books in Italy and abroad. She holds workshops for children and adults, collaborating with schools and libraries. In recent years, she has beautifully illustrated several books for White Star Kids.

White Star Kids® is a registered trademark property of White Star s.r.l.

© 2022 White Star s.r.l.
Piazzale Luigi Cadorna, 6
20123 Milan, Italy
www.whitestar.it

Translation: TperTradurre S.r.l., Rome
Editing: Michele Suchomel-Casey

All rights reserved. No part of this publication may be reproduced, stored or transmitted in any form or by any means without written permission from the publisher.

First printing, February 2022

ISBN 978-88-544-1862-2
1 2 3 4 5 6   26 25 24 23 22

Printed and manufactured in Serbia by Grafostil

P. 9: CLARA'S EGGS

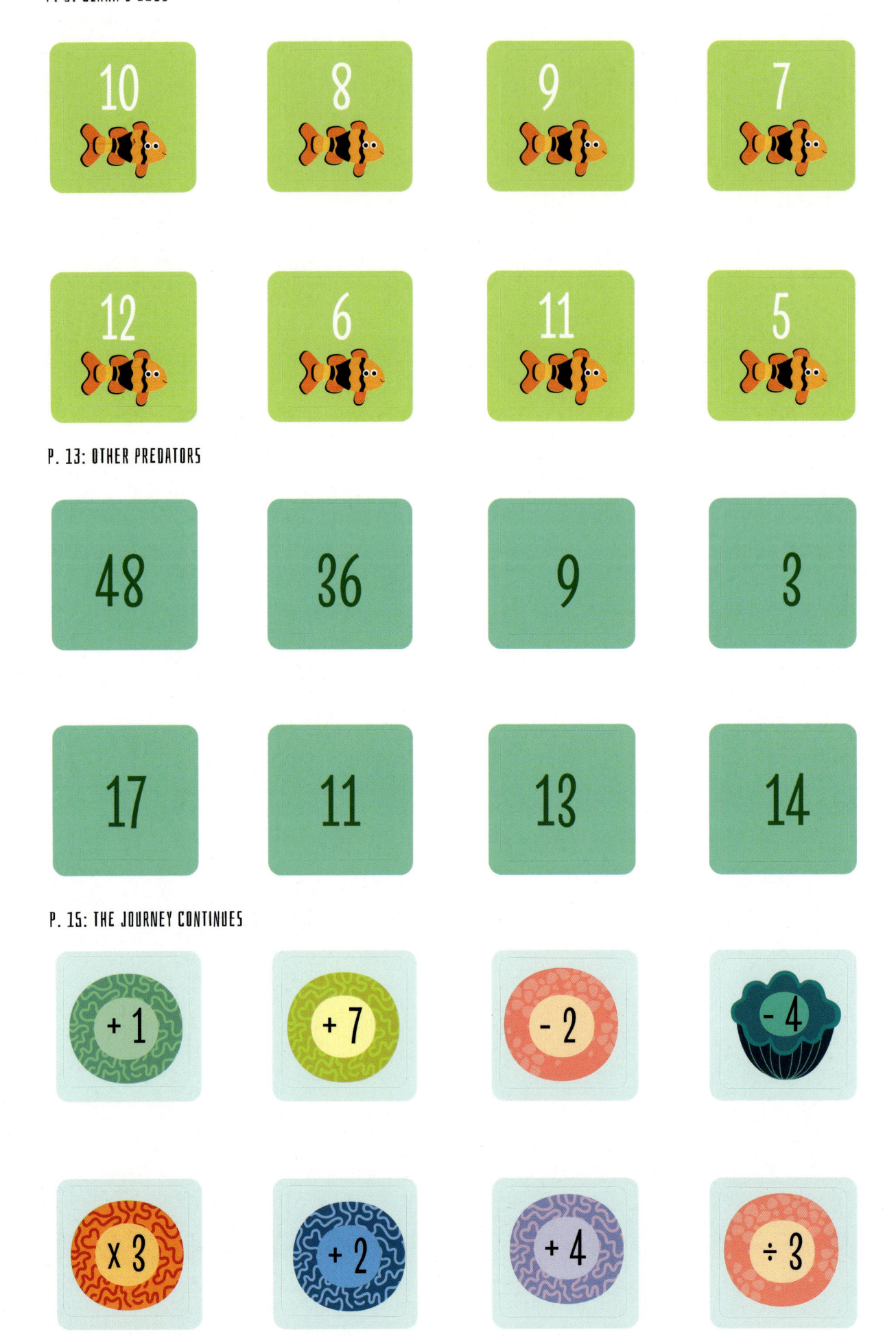

10	8	9	7
12	6	11	5

P. 13: OTHER PREDATORS

48	36	9	3
17	11	13	14

P. 15: THE JOURNEY CONTINUES

+ 1	+ 7	− 2	− 4
× 3	+ 2	+ 4	÷ 3

PP. 20-21: FORM YOUR TEAMS

PP. 26-27 TIME FOR THE TONGUE FISH GAME!

PP. 26-27 TIME FOR THE TONGUE FISH GAME!

P. 28 THE SUPREME COURT

6 15 3 4

P. 33: SPLOTCHES IN THE SQUARE

PP. 34-35: CRYPTIC CHOREOGRAPHIES

PP. 36-37: COUNT THE MISSING SEA CREATURES

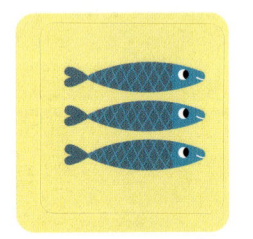

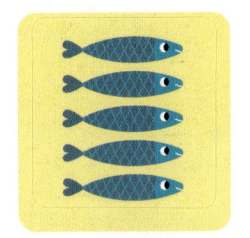

PP. 38-39: THE MYSTERY OF KING PLAICE

2	5	6	3
14	1	10	14
11	16	13	7

P. 41: THE PATH BETWEEN THE BUBBLES

PP. 48-49: THE PROPHECY

	33	23	
13	15	8	10
7		66	53
4	20	5	
19	3	6	51
	8	2	97

P. 50: THE FINAL TEST

P. 51: CONGRATULATIONS!